*me,*

*for us,"*

*Foreword by David McDaniel*

*Bill Yount*

# Some Hear Thunder…
# I Hear a Roar!

## Supernatural Encounters &
## Stories to Encourage Your Heart

By Bill Yount

Published by
Blowing the Shofar Ministries
132 E. North Ave.
Hagerstown, MD 21740
*www.billyount.com*

Unless otherwise noted, all Scripture verses are taken from the Authorized King James Version (KJV) of the Bible. Public domain in the U.S.A.

Scripture references marked NIV are taken from The Holy Bible, New International Version NIV, copyright © 1973,1978, 1984, 2011 by International Bible Society, Colorado Springs, Colorado.

Scripture quotations marked MSG are taken from The Message, Copyright © 1993, 1994, 1995, 1996, 2000, 2001, 2002. Used by permission.

Scripture quotations marked NASB are taken from the New American Standard Bible, Copyright © 1960, 1962, 1963, 1968, 1971, 1972, 1973, 1975, 1977, 1995 by The Lockman Foundation. Used by permission.

ISBN-13: 978-1530207336
ISBN-10: 1530207339

Cover Design by Thomas Griffin
Printed in the United States of America
For Worldwide Distribution

# Endorsements

*"Some Hear thunder... I Hear a Roar!* This book is a timely word for the body of Christ right now. Get ready to see greater signs and wonders manifested by the power of the Spirit as you dive deep into the wells of wisdom and revelation in this beautiful manuscript."

Lana Vawser
Itinerant speaker,
prophetic voice and author of *"Desperately Deep"*

"The very best teachers and the most effective prophets have one thing in common: they use personal and fascinating stories to convey their message. My personal friend, Bill Yount, goes way, way, WAY beyond fascinating stories in this amazing book of his life journey on hearing God personally speak. He uses stories beyond number—and these stories will teach YOU to hear God's Voice today!

Frankly, you're going to love this book and have a hard time putting it down as the zeal of the Lord consumes you. Like Bill says, and you will experience, "I live to hear God speak. My worst days have taught me when God speaks, you live! When God speaks, you're healed! When God speaks, you're delivered! Storm clouds scatter. Dead dreams thunder with life!

Get this book, folks. One for you, and one for a friend, please!"

Steve Shultz
Founder, THE ELIJAH LIST

"Bill Yount ministers from a place of authenticity and passion to see others come to know the power of God at work in their lives. We've received testimony after testimony of lives impacted and changed for the Gory of God through Bill's writing. We believe in His ministry and that it is the Lord's heart exposed and hands extended to touch the earth. We have featured Bill's articles on *Spirit Fuel* since the inception of our platform, and hope to continue to do so for many years to come."

Joel Yount and Thomas Griffin
Co-Founders of *Spirit Fuel*

*"When I call to remembrance the unfeigned faith*
*that is in thee, which dwelt first in thy grandmother Lois,*
*and thy mother, Eunice; and I am persuaded*
*that in thee also."(2 Timothy 1:5).*

## Dedication

"Some Hear Thunder... I Hear a Roar!" is being dedicated to my mother, Gertrude Yount, who went to be with Jesus on March 2, 2015. She was ninety years old. She now knows what it's like to run her fingers through the mane of the lion that walked with her throughout this life... The Lion of the tribe of Judah.

The Lion of the Tribe of Judah is a symbolic reference to Jesus Christ. The lion is the symbol for the Jewish tribe of Judah, one of the twelve tribes of Israel named after the twelve sons of Jacob. Judah, the third son, whose name means thanks and praise, was the royal line from which King David and eventually our Messiah, Jesus Christ was born. This royal line was established under the covenant God made with Abraham. We see this reference in Revelation 5:2, 4-5:

> *"And I saw a strong angel proclaiming with a loud voice, Who is worthy to open the book, and to loose the seals thereof? And I wept much because no man was found worthy to open and to read the book thereon. And one of the elders saith unto me, Weep not: behold, the **Lion of the tribe of Judah**, the Root of David, hath prevailed to open the book, and to loose the seven seals thereof."*

Jesus, the sinless One from the tribe of Judah, is the only One found worthy!

# *Acknowledgments*

First of all I want to thank you, Lord, for making all things possible, including this book

Thanks to my beautiful wife, Dagmar, for allowing me to have the time to pursue this project.

A special thank you to my mother, Gertrude and my father, Clifford who are watching from above and cheering their children on.

Thank you, Cheryl Jenkins, Founder of *Kingdom One Business Solutions*, for working late into the night to edit my book. Without your gift of organization and advice it wouldn't have survived.

A special thanks to Thomas Griffin, co-founder of *Spirit Fuel*, who created what I saw in the Spirit for the front and back cover of this book. What a gift of creativity the Lord has given you.

Thank you, *Bridge of Life*, my home church, where I have attended for almost 39 years as of now. You have loved and supported our family these many years.

I am honored to be a member of the *Apostolic Company of Alliance International Ministries*. Thank you for speaking into my life and encouraging me to step into my purpose without fear.

Finally, I want to thank all of my friends, and those we have never met, who have loved and prayed my family through our most difficult times in life. Because of you we are still here and we will overcome by the Blood of the Lamb and the word of our testimony.

# Table of Contents

# *Foreword*

As we travel throughout the short pathway of our lifetime, it is surrounded with myriads of tests, tribulations, and truths. In these daily challenges, we are faced with a choice of how we perceive them. If we look at them at face value, we can devalue their purpose. On the other hand, if we embrace them in light of God's truth, our eyes can see the love of God toward us in each one. This book depicts how important it is to lay a foundation of honor at the base of our climb, and upon it our walk is embedded with plateaus of God's truth as both our training ground and our safety net. Bill expresses this honor for his parents in this book, and his stories and messages create a safe place for us to garner these truths and apply them to our lives. God is up to something pretty big, and He is using all of us if we will just surrender our vulnerabilities and insecurities to Him.

Bill is my friend, and he has had an impact on my life as I started out in ministry as he released the sound of the shofar. I appreciate his willingness to step out into uncharted waters in obedience reflected in the many stories in this book. While some stories are reflections of how God has used his life, all of them carry a prophetic undertone of what God is saying to us. Enjoy the stories and antidotes as you apply them to your walk with God and your journey with others.

Dave McDaniel - Men of Issachar
Director, Aglow International
Author of *Stepping out of the Boat, Dancing on the Waters*

# *Introduction*

A lion roared inside my mother's womb: "I have called you to be a prophet to the nations!" Who am I that the King of the Universe would think of me in this way? The wonder of this call still remains a mystery to me. Revelation of it flashes before me like lightning at times and despite my worst days, the call rings loud and clear, never changing. It's who God says I am!

When you know what God has called you to do, nothing can stop you... but yourself. I still never quite get used to ministering to people or typing out a message, but as time moves on, the butterflies are fewer and my knees are not so weak. The call of God reminds me I can do this. This is what I was born for and the greater One is in me. The roar of an untamed lion is in my call.

I will never forget the day an apostle spoke over me, "Bill, it's not your fault that you're a prophet. But you have to walk in it." Don't apologize for the call of God on your life either. Walk in it and let the lion roar!

How thankful I am for those who encourage me as I continue to grow in the things of God and in the prophetic. And most of all for His assurance: "The words that you speak will be greater than who you are."

## I Live to Hear God Speak

The first time God spoke to me personally, I didn't know it was Him. I thought it was my mother. When I was five years old she would tell everybody, "This is my little preacher!" It embarrassed me at the time. But looking back, it was God speaking through her. Thirty-six years into ministry, I am still preaching. Though humbling, the Lord will often speak to us through the least likely people. This is part of our training before we can hear His voice for ourselves. The Lord uses unique vessels. Like iron that sharpens iron, they often are the keys that unlock our spiritual ears.

As a new Christian, out of the gate running, hell took its best shot at me to abort the innate desire to ever hear God's voice. A wedge of contention drove deep between my Bible teacher and myself the moment he said, "God spoke to me." Those words were alien to me. Immediately, my whole being was flooded with doubts as the enemy unleashed those infamous fatal words: *"Indeed, has God said?"* (Genesis 3:1). Surely this man had a big ego problem thinking God Almighty would take the time to speak to him personally among the billions of people on earth. I left the Bible study in frustration that evening thinking he was certainly out of his mind. That crazy teacher kept me awake. An hour later a question walked into my bedroom, "But what if you could? What if you could actually hear God speak to you?" As I began to faintly consider the possibility of an answer, that question lit a fire within me that has never gone out. I thought to myself, if God could actually speak to me, I would be willing to wait thirty or forty years to hear Him speak one word, not a whole sentence, but just one word.

Two hours later, the Lord himself walked into my sleepless night. He said, "Son, I want to speak to you more than you want Me to." From that moment in my journey I began listening for His voice. Now you know what I live for. I live to hear God speak. My worst days have taught me when God speaks, you live! When God speaks, you're healed! When God speaks, you're delivered! Storm clouds scatter. Dead dreams thunder with life! I'm not talking about man speaking but when God speaks, you live! His voice has brought me through hell and back, changing doctors' reports and adding years to my life. The devil's best shot missed me.

# *Tribute*

Mom made us go to church. "You are going," she said. "As long as you are under our roof, you will be under the roof of God's house!" Before I knew the Lord, I thanked Him that our church had a balcony. It didn't matter to Mom where we sat as long as we were under that roof. We perched on the highest and farthest seats from the pulpit. We talked and carried on with friends and got away with a lot of things, or so we thought. Then one Sunday morning, a lady from the pulpit started to sing, "He Touched Me." I suddenly discovered how long God's arm is. It's at least as long as the pulpit is from the balcony, for He touched me. I walked away from my friends and with weak knees, started down the side steps of the balcony. I walked down the center aisle of the church while she was still singing, and made my way to the altar. The Lord is the only person I know Who can interrupt His own church service and not get upset. I gave my life to the Lord that day, and I have never been the same since.

At eleven years of age my mother often attended Kathryn Kuhlman meetings in Pittsburgh, PA. She saw unusual happenings that forever changed her life. A huge goiter on her mother's neck instantly disappeared before her eyes. The next second a five year old boy began jumping up and down shouting, "Mommy, where are you? Where are you, Mommy?" The mother on the other side of the boy said, "Honey, I'm right here." Mom said, "I saw that little boy jump up into his mother's arms and began shouting, "Oh mommy, I can see you! I can see you,

Mommy!" The mother cried, "He was born blind!"

At that moment my mother received a new mindset: "This is the way my life is going to be," and it continued throughout her life. Little did she know that what she experienced in those miracle meetings would one day cause healing to run in her own life and family.

# Section One

# The Roar in Our Family Legacy

# Healing Still Runs in My Family

As a result of this new mindset, Mom saw many miracles in her life. She was diagnosed with cancer forty-five years ago. It was spreading throughout her body with a death sentence of five years. Mom felt led to visit a different church in town. She went with Aunt Sophie who has been healed so many times that people thought she was crazy. If you are believing for a miracle or healing, be careful who you hang out with. You better find two or three crazy people who believe "all things are possible!" They arrived early and sat near the front of the church before others got there. As soon as Mom sat down, she felt a hand touch her shoulder, shooting a bolt of electricity down through her body as it burned the hairs off her arms. "I just knew God healed me of that cancer!" she said. They found out later that church didn't believe in healing. I think that's why God healed her before the service started. That cancer never came back on Mom. She loved to tell people of her healings and miracles. Then she would stop and say, "But you gotta repent!" as conviction fell on them.

Then a tumor appeared on Mom's thyroid. Doctors wanted to test it for cancer. Mom prayed the night before the test. "Lord, if I get weak and sick with this tumor, how am I going to help anybody?" While she was on the table the doctor held a needle in one hand and felt for the tumor with the other. Again he felt for the tumor. After a moment of silence, the doctor said, "Mrs. Yount, I can't take this test. I can't find the tumor. It's gone!" Mom said, "I shimmied off the table and staggered down the hallway under the power of God like a drunkard. The Great Physician beat the doctors to it."

When in her 70s, Mom faced a quadruple bypass surgery. I prayed for her the night before. She then prayed for herself. Her prayer was so short it concerned me. She didn't even say "Amen." I wanted to tell her she should pray longer for the seriousness of this surgery, but I didn't. I will never forget her short prayer that night. She prayed, "Lord, tomorrow morning is one of the reasons I've served You my whole life." That was it. She came through that surgery with flying colors.

When she turned 80 years old, she was working in an assisted living home taking care of older people. She told us, "All these people are old in here." A couple years later, her family doctor said, "What we have found this time, you will have to quit your job and stop driving your car." He shouldn't have touched mom's car. With the doctor's report, Mom had to quit her job and the state took her license. Mom called me one night and said, "Bill, my best friends are calling me to encourage me but they end up reminding me of all my problems. I told them all, 'I don't have any problems, I just keep going.'"

The following Sunday she went to church to be anointed and prayed for by the elders. She called me that Sunday evening and said, "They anointed me with oil and prayed. I believe God healed me again and I want my license back!" Mom started calling up her doctors every other day demanding another test for her illness. She finally wore one doctor out. He gave her another test. As he read the test results with my Mother sitting in his office, he stopped halfway through the report and looked at her; "Mrs. Yount, I think you can go back to work now." Mom said, "How am I going to get there?" The doctor said, "Let me see what I can do." Mom did get her license back and drove again. This is unheard of at mom's age of eighty-two years. But I am learning when you get a breakthrough or victory, it's preparation for what is to come. The next test was right around the corner.

**Mom's Foot Totally Healed**

I remember when the doctor wanted to amputate mom's foot. It all started when our family received a shocking call saying our mother had fallen down the basement steps and broke her ankle severely. Through surgery, they put eleven pins and a plate in her ankle, but because of her battle with diabetes, her ankle refused to heal. The doctors finally said, "Mrs. Yount, if the ankle does not begin to heal in a couple weeks, we are considering amputation." But I believe God heard her faith-filled, childlike prayer. "Lord, you don't need my foot, and I do."

They marked mom's leg and explained about the artificial foot and said, "You'll get along fine with it." But Mom prophesied to the doctors, "Whenever I go to Heaven, I am taking my foot with me!" Mom often told her doctors "Who" was in the process of healing her so that when it happened they knew they had very little to do with it. Weeks went by with no healing. The doctors told the family, "The foot is dead. It is black and has no circulation in it. You can take her anywhere else, but it's too late."

If you have been given a "no hope" report from a doctor, I strongly recommend you get a second opinion. The Lord led my Mother to a doctor in Pittsburgh, PA for a second opinion, and I went with Mom to see this doctor. As he looked at mom's foot he said, "I'm going to try a couple things," and he walked out of the room. I followed him out and asked what he really thought. He said, "I believe there's hope."

I never heard those words from any of her other doctors. His words encouraged the whole family. I stayed the following week for Mom's surgery. As the doctors came into her room that night to give her the report, the lead doctor said, "Mrs. Yount, I believe when you go to Heaven, you will be taking your foot with you." This surgeon took the eleven pins and plate back out! After a battle of believing for five long months, along with special therapy, Mom's foot was totally healed.

At eighty-two years old, Mom was living in an assisted living home where she used to work years ago. She was battling some health problems but she still gets around well, going to church on Sundays, and still lives to help others. One day she told the director, "I don't know why I am here in this place, for God has healed me so many times before." The director's son spoke up and said, "Maybe God sent you here to tell us about Him."

At eighty-seven, a second cancer was removed through surgery. They got it all with no chemo needed. Most doctors who told her she wouldn't live long are gone. She kept outliving her doctors and diseases. Her wisdom is outlasting her enemies and mine, too.

# An Unstoppable Persevering Faith

When it came to loving people, mom broke the rules. I remember as a young boy when she took us five kids to church, she always squeezed other people into the car with us, like sardines. Most Sundays she would pick up a woman and her three kids, which made ten of us in the car. Many times we would hear mom holler at us kids in the back seat, "Get down! There's a policeman!" She seemed to get away with some things when she was helping people.

Late in life, my mother had an ulcer on her leg that wasn't healing because of her diabetes. Doctors discovered the main artery in her leg was one hundred percent blocked with plaque that prevented the healing. Two doctors wouldn't touch it because she was 90 years old. A third doctor said, "I'm going to try it." (Sometimes we need to try some things that look impossible.) He told my sister, "I chiseled it. I kept chiseling it. Two days later he called my sister and said, "The blood is flowing!"

When I heard those words, I sensed the Lord saying to the Body of Christ. "The blood is flowing! The blood is flowing! I've been chiseling away at the blockages in your life. The blood is beginning to flow into the legs of My Body." The life is in the blood. Strength in our legs is coming from that blood. We are going to walk in newness of life, walk in places we have never been, do things we have never done and try some things that look impossible.

Mom was a fighter. *'A contender of the faith that was once delivered to the saints.'* (Jude 1:3) She fought for what she got.

Her strong faith was like a runaway freight train that could not be stopped. Mom was four-feet, eleven-inches tall, but in the Spirit she could take out Muhammad Ali. She seemed to have the gift of faith. But there were times and seasons when God seemed distant, when the healings and miracles weren't arriving on time. Yet, her faith kept going. Mom's answer to heaven's silence was: "I'll be ok. Let's see what God will do." It was these bumps in the road of mom's life that caused her to know the Lord like she did. Her life taught me there's a whole lot of living between healings and miracles. And a whole lot of living after them. She knew how to run this race of life with patience.

> *"Wherefore seeing we also are compassed about with so great a cloud of witnesses, let us lay aside every weight, and the sin which doth so easily beset us, and let us run with patience the race that is set before us."* (Hebrews 12:1)

She ran with patience. Patience was her friend.

# When the Lion Roars, His Call is Not Tame

Check out Moses, Abraham, Jonah, the twelve disciples, and anyone walking with God today. You will see the divine interruptions that plummeted their lives. At twenty-one years of age I began working in a steel mill near Pittsburgh, Pennsylvania. My goal was to save money to get married one day. Within a short time, things were looking up; I owned a new car, paid for in cash. Everything was coming into view except someone to marry.

After several more years of accumulating a sizable bank account for my dream, a voice spoke to me: "Lay down your nets and follow Me." I was certain that was not God. He would have known it takes money to get married. Besides, I was sure the Lord blessed me with this good paying job with great benefits and a secure future. As time went by it became clear, however, it was God knocking on the door of that factory.

"Son, lay down your nets and follow Me." I dragged my feet on those words for two more years, knowing that call could greatly hinder my dream from coming true. One day while eating lunch in the work yard, I saw, in the spirit, Jesus walking past the factory. He didn't stop but kept walking as He pointed to me and said, "Son, I'm calling you for the very last time!" I knew it was now or never. I could stay where I was and be a light in that factory. But I knew I would miss knowing Jesus the way the disciples did when they left their nets and followed Him.

Two weeks later, I handed in my resignation. The guys I worked with thought I was crazy for leaving a good paying job. They kept asking me, "What are you going to do when your money runs out and you do find someone to marry? I didn't have an answer. All I knew was that God was calling me out of the factory and not telling me what my next step in life would be. All I could say to my co-workers was, "God is calling me to leave and He promised He would take care of me."

Thirty days after I left the factory, it began to shut down permanently and it never reopened. I knew then the Lord didn't call me because I was so spiritual. He was looking out for me. What I thought was my security wasn't. He saw the hole in the bottom of my boat. Will the call of God interrupt your life? Definitely! If necessary, it may close down a whole factory, business, or even your present ministry when the call comes knocking on your door. It often comes roaring like an untamed lion. The call can be wild.

**The Roar Will Often Cause You to Do Things Backwards**

My life Scripture was born in that factory: *"By faith Abraham, when called to go to a place he would later receive as his inheritance, obeyed and went, even though he did not know where he was going."* (Hebrews 11:8, NIV) The Lord wasn't telling me what to do next, but I knew He was calling me. He began stirring my nest at home also.

While working in the factory, on occasion I would visit my brother, Jim, in Maryland. I experienced God's peace there. After leaving the factory at the end of seven years, I sensed the Lord leading me to leave home and move in with my brother and his family. My brother began taking me to prayer meetings. I discovered something strange. I met the poorest Christians in the state of Maryland. Almost everyone in those meetings had a financial need. After several prayer meetings and many financial requests, the Lord spoke to me: "I want to talk to you about My money in your bank account. Since I haven't given you someone to marry yet, you won't be needing it right now. But others do."

The next prayer meeting a man shared a need of several thousand dollars. I thought I had better give to this request before I heard of a larger one. At my brother's home that night I secretly wrote out the largest check in my life. As I wrote the check, I felt like a saw was cutting on my shoulder blade. Many years of hard earned money was now escaping me through the tip of a pen. The Lord led me to give the check to a pastor to give to the man in need so he would never know where it came from. I didn't get to share any glory in my giving.

I have noticed something walking with the Lord. When I obey what He says, He continues to speak to me. But it's not always what I want to hear. Thirty days after I moved into my brother's home, the Lord spoke: "I didn't call you to leave your father and mother and cleave to your brother. I am calling you alone to know Me." I explained to my brother what God had said. I packed up everything I owned in my car and drove slowly out of my brother's driveway. All I knew was that God called me from the factory, from my parent's home, and now from my brother and his family.

Pulling onto Interstate 70, doubts flooded my mind. The devil shouted. "What are you going to do now if you do find someone to marry? How will you survive?" I had to answer that voice before I could continue on. I said, "Devil, if Jesus doesn't do one more thing for me other than what He did at Calvary, I will still follow Him!" Dead silence. The subject was never brought up again.

## Hagerstown, Maryland

I held tight to my life Scripture message: *"By faith Abraham [Bill Yount] obeyed and went, even though he did not know where he was going"* (Hebrews 11:8). After driving for a while, I saw an exit sign to Hagerstown, Maryland. I had never been there before. I just happened to take that exit. Looking back, I know God knows how to drive an automobile. Since I had no agenda of my own, it was easier for Him to guide me. I drove into the center of the city and parked the car. Walking down an alley I discovered a Christian coffeehouse there. I walked inside and the Bible teacher was teaching on "Abraham going out, not knowing where He was going." Hmm...very interesting!

From the time I arrived in Hagerstown, Maryland, a spirit of giving came upon me. I actually wanted to give my money away wherever I saw a need. This had to be God. I remember one Sunday morning in church there; I had just three one dollar bills left. As the offering plate was being passed, I put my last bit of money in. It was the first time in my life I was without any resources. That Sunday evening the pastor was preaching and stopped mid-stream. He said, "There is someone here who has left everything to follow Jesus. The Lord wants you to know that He is going to meet your needs according to His riches in glory by Christ Jesus!" A bolt of electricity surged all through my being as it did right now writing this. The lion was roaring loud and clear.

From that moment on, I began to see the Lord's provision for my life. I have learned that when God calls a man or woman, He calls for everything, including the wallet and purse, before He can trust us with spiritual riches. I can tell you why I had to leave everything; it was so I could find my future wife, and I did. She was where God was leading me to the whole time.

After a year and a half of getting to know each other, we set a wedding date. I had no money. Neither did she. But the Lord had been preparing both of us for years to live by faith. We had no furniture or housekeeping supplies of our own, but we knew the Lord was bringing us together for marriage. I was living in an apartment at the time and volunteering for a prison ministry. The Lord was providing in unusual ways to pay the rent and meet my daily needs.

Two months before our wedding date, the Lion of the Tribe of Judah roared the loudest I had ever heard Him up to that time. I was singing in a little country church, and a friend was preaching a revival there. A man came up after the service and asked my friend if he knew of anyone who could use a bedroom suite. They had it in the paper to sell, but it didn't sell so they felt led to bless someone by giving it away. My preacher friend explained that I was getting married in a couple of months and I was believing the Lord to provide what we would need. The man delivered it to my apartment. It was a three piece cherry bedroom suite!

A week later the man called me and invited myself and my future wife, Dagmar, to their home in Winchester, Virginia. They began sharing their testimony with us. They said, "God is calling us to go to Bible school out west and we are unable to take everything with us. He is showing us that He is going to take care of us as we go. And besides that, He has told us to give you everything in our house!" I looked at Dagmar and said, "If this is a dream, don't wake me!" They gave everything from their furniture, washer and dryer, down to the cereal boxes in their cupboards! It was worth far more than what I had tried to save in my measly bank account. Our apartment couldn't hold it all. We had to give some things away.

I said, "Lord, why are You going overboard in blessing us like this?" He said, "Son, when you were willing to lay down your nets and follow Me and die to your dream by giving your bank account away, My Word promises: *"Give and it shall be given unto you; good measure, pressed down, and shaken together, and running over, shall men give into your bosom..."* (Luke 6:38). We have been married thirty-four years, and have three children and two grandchildren. I have been young and I am getting older. But I have never seen the righteous forsaken nor their seed begging bread. I have heard my children cry out to God at times, but they have never begged for bread.

The Lord is our provider and He never forgets what we give to Him. One day the Lord spoke to me, "Son, remember when you were seven years old and they stood you and your sister on a chair behind the pulpit and you sang for Me?" I said, "Yes, Lord." He said, "I am going to bless you both in the near future for that. I never forget what you do for Me. It never goes unrewarded."

# Section Two

# Words of Encouragement

# Overlooked Treasure

Have we overlooked the treasure in older people in rest homes? One time, I visited my mother in an assisted living center. There, I met an eighty something year old missionary to the Indians. She showed us photos of her life story and a newspaper article about her mother who was blind for sixteen years and suddenly could see. This sister shared how one day she hugged her mother and said, "Lord, I want momma to see." Suddenly her mother got her sight back.

She went on to tell other stories of how she had the gift of healing for many people. I said to her, "Would you pray for me? I have a bone spur that still gives me pain." Before she prayed, she said, "You will feel heat in my right hand as I touch your neck. And you will be fine in the morning." That night I slept without pain and it has never come back. While I was among these older people the Lord said to me. "I am giving you the wisdom of the ancient. Thanks for visiting Me."

> *"With the ancient is wisdom; and in length of days understanding."* (Job 12:12)

# God Is Calling Forth the 'Edge Pushers'

I sense the Father saying, "I am going to do fearless exploits with those who are 'wired' different. Some will seem to have 'no wiring' at all. They will be famous for not being normal because they weren't born normal. They were born to push the edge back off of their families, cities and nations. They will also push the edge back and break off every limitation that My present day church has put on itself.

"I am sending these 'unique ones' who will be the forerunners in routing every religious spirit out of My House. They will break the rules when it comes to reaching the lost. But don't judge them. You may be shaking your head 'no' to the next move of My fearless exploits in reaching the harvest." If you've ever felt 'not normal', 'wired different', or have 'no wiring' at all. You may be in this sacred number.

> *"But God hath chosen the foolish things of the world to confound the wise; and God hath chosen the weak things of the world to confound the things which are mighty;"* (1 Corinthians 1:27).

# Plan on God Using You, Like Never Before

God is going to use you like never before. Make plans for it. If the Lord has called you to write, write; if it's painting, paint or if speaking, speak. If doors don't open for you to speak anywhere, go out in the woods and speak to the trees. You will soon see trees as men walking. Speak to the mountains and you will start seeing them move, even in your own life. Billy Graham started by preaching to cows. God plans on using you this year like no other generation.

The first reason is: The Lord needs you more than ever in a world that is falling apart. The second reason: The lost will be calling on you, asking you to give the reason for the hope that is in you. The Lord is sending His angels to loose you into the harvest fields with your gifts and talents. Don't worry about having enough training. Your trusting in the Lord will be your training. Make your plans now. It's time.

# God is Renaming You; Your New Name Shall Be Called 'CONFIDENCE.'

Before getting up to minister recently, my wife sensed that I was battling intimidation. She leaned over to me and whispered, "Your new name is 'Confidence!' Immediately, a lion roared on the inside of me and an alarm went off in hell. I rose up to minister and the Lion of the Tribe of Judah took over the meeting.

I believe the Lord is renaming you today. Your new name is 'Confidence'! "You shall no longer be called wounded, outcast, lonely or afraid. You shall be called 'Confidence, Joyfulness, Overcoming One, Faithfulness, Friend of God. One who seeks My face." (Lyrics from *I Will Change Your Name* by D.J. Butler).[1]

Get up and let the lion roar.

*"It will no longer be said to you, "Forsaken," Nor to your land will it any longer be said, "Desolate"; But you will be called, "My delight is in her," And your land, "Married"; For the LORD delights in you, and to Him your land will be married."* (Isaiah 62:4 NASB).

---

1   Butler, D.J., *I Will Change Your Name*; 1987, Anaheim Vineyard Publishing.

# When God Calls

When God calls He rarely considers our plans. Where He leads often makes no sense. When I want to stay, He says, "Go!" When I want to go, He says, "Stay!" The worst place on earth turns out to be perfect to advance His kingdom. And He never asks me what time it is when He says, "Go!"

## Tomato Salvation

A husband and wife shared how they wanted to leave their small town in Texas. Darkness oppressed them. God said, "Stay and plant a church!" They did. A woman, also known as the town drunk, kept interrupting the services. She stomped her feet and gave mean looks. The pastor, while preaching, happened to mention how he loved tomatoes. The intoxicated woman with a loud voice spoke up. "Tomatoes? I grow tomatoes in my back yard. I will bring you some!" The next service she brought the tomatoes. During the sermon she came under conviction and gave her life to the Lord. Instant deliverance! The whole town shook from the power of her testimony. Her drinking friends still ask her. "How long is this going to last?" She tells them. "Til Jesus comes and for all eternity. I am done with alcohol. I have no taste for it!" When God calls us to a certain place, it usually isn't for our sake but for someone else's

## God's Most Wanted List

When God calls, it's time to tear up our list of people who we think are too far gone in sin and evil. Surprisingly, we find them on "God's Most Wanted List," where we used to be. If God saved you and me, He can save anybody. I believe when we see God face to face, we will realize we could have loved more and judged less.

> *"Moreover the law entered, that the offense might abound. But where sin abounded, grace did much more abound."* (Romans 5:20).

# Spread Your Broken Wings and Fly

*"If your heart is broken, you'll find God right there; if you're kicked in the gut, He'll help you catch your breath."* (Psalm 34:18 The Message Bible).

Broken is defined as "having been fractured or damaged and no longer in one piece or in working order (of a person) having given up all hope; despairing." It seems no matter who we are and how much we love Jesus, there's still a broken area in our lives that God is still working on. I said to my wife recently, "Do you know anyone in the Body of Christ, including us, who's not broken in some area of their lives? Do you know anyone who is normal?" She said, "Bill, normal is the setting on the dryer downstairs."

## I'm In Your Brokenness

I sense an urgent cry from God's heart: "Wait no longer. I'm in your brokenness when things didn't go the way you planned, and I didn't answer the way you thought I would. So broken, you felt like a bird without wings. But I'm still here, and you are under My wings. Would you do Me a favor? Spread your broken wings one more time. Give Me one more chance. See what I can do, for I am breathing on your brokenness. Can you feel My breath?"

"I've waited for you to cry out to me; only Me. Let Me be your dream now, and I will take you to My dream that I have for you. Try it. One more time. Spread your broken wings and see where they will take you. I will be the wind that carries you above the storms, pain, and sorrow. It's your time to defy gravity. At first it may hurt again, but it will not harm you now. You will laugh again, dance again, and love again. Spread your broken wings and make history."

### Did Our Brokenness Come to Define Us?

Nothing is wasted in the hands of our Redeemer. All things work together for our good to those who love the Lord. That means even our pain, disappointments, and things that don't make sense. Could it be that we've tasted brokenness in order to relate to a broken world and to have our heart break for it? Can you feel them: broken hearts, broken dreams, broken hopes, and broken bones? Maybe we should take a year and weep with those that weep. There must be an ocean of tears somewhere bottled by God's hand ready to be redeemed.

Lord, let this be the year we find You. A year where our dream that's coming true is You, so we can get over ourselves and heal a broken, dying world. Lord, begin with me. Weep through me over Jerusalem. Weep through me for the lost. I wonder when we stand before You if we will regret that we didn't weep more on earth. Not for ourselves or for the things that didn't work out, but for those who didn't make it there with us. We will have all eternity to rejoice and be glad. Lord, is that tear in my eye mine or Yours?

### A Year to Hear Tears Falling

"I'm opening the ears of My people to hear tears falling this year. You will hear tears splashing, hitting the ground so hard that they will erode mountains and make rivers out of deserts. If you run from them, they will pursue you until you can hear nothing else." Just as the prophet Elijah told the widow to go borrow many vessels, I hear the Father saying, "Go borrow many bottles, for there will be more tears than there are bottles on the earth. Tears from orphans pounding against gross darkness, screaming, 'Can anyone hear me?' You will hear widows plead in the night for their cruse of oil not to fail. You will hear children imprisoned in sex-trafficking with no more tears left to cry, staring into outer space; a tearless generation robbed of their emotions. There will be older people in rest homes weeping for the younger generations, that they might learn from their long life of taking the road less traveled. Is not wisdom found among the aged? Does not long life bring understanding? (See Job 12:12.) You may need to visit them to hear their heart's cry."

Perhaps when we weep with those who weep, our brokenness begins to heal and our broken wings will want to fly again to those whose weeping is greater than our own. Our broken wings must fly, not for our own sake, but for God's sake. I saw a little bird recently flying high in the sky with strong winds blowing against it. I said to the Lord, "How can that small bird fly against those fierce winds?" The Lord said, "They were born that way. They were created to fly in winds of adversity. And so are you."

Have the violent winds of life knocked you down? They were blowing hard against you to go higher in God. Have you forgotten that you were born to fly in spite of them? Are you wondering where your wings are? They are beginning to grow now. By faith begin to stretch them. You can do it. Hear the tears of others falling. They need you now. Go ahead. Stretch your broken wings and change history.

# A Season of Wondering, "Have I Lost Jesus Somewhere?"

We all have those times when we wonder, "Have I lost Jesus somewhere?" Even Jesus' own parents, Mary and Joseph, lost Him for three whole days and couldn't find Him. *"But they, supposing him to have been in the company, went a day's journey; and they sought him among their kinsfolk and acquaintance."* (Luke 2:44). What a shock especially for Mary to have birthed the treasure of the world and wonder where He was. *"And it came to pass, that, after three days, they found him in the temple."* (Luke 2:46) At twelve years of age He was about His Father's business to save you and me. It's easy to lose Jesus in a crowded world. If it seems you have lost Him, be encouraged. He is about to make His grand entrance into your life. But, you may have to take a journey.

When God says, "Come away, My Beloved," a million "Likes" on Facebook won't satisfy. You crave to see His face. And it doesn't matter then if your favorite sports team wins or loses, for the things of this world grow strangely dim. People will say, "That was one of the best messages I've ever heard," but you felt nothing. And you were the speaker. When He bids you come, your fingers go numb and your passion to write dies. You can do nothing without Him. We live by faith and not by sight or feelings, but sooner or later, if His presence doesn't return, you will check your pulse wondering, "Did I lose Jesus somewhere?"

Your hunger grows. You eat off other people's plates during

church now. Someone whispers after the service, "I didn't get a thing out of that pastor's message." You tell them, "It's because I got it all. I was so hungry I ate off your plate!" Unfamiliar scriptures come alive. "To the hungry soul, every bitter thing tastes sweet." (Proverbs 27:7). You get so hungry for God, you eat giants. They become your nourishment. They come for only one reason: to strengthen you. For you are on a quest to find God again. On the way the ravens feed you; people you thought God could never use are the ones keeping you alive now. With eyes straining, you start seeing God in everyone. He puts something you need in the person you don't like. Surprisingly, it's now your enemy telling you where your next meal is. And you love him for it.

Your stomach growls. Like the four lepers in Samaria in the time of famine, you're starving.

*"And there were four leprous men at the entering in of the gate of Samaria: and they said one to another, Why sit we here until we die? If we say, we will enter into the city, then the famine is in the city, and we shall die there: and if we sit still here, we die also. Now therefore come, and let us fall unto the host of the Syrians: if they save us alive, we shall live; and if they kill us, we shall but die."* (2 Kings 7:3, 4).

You are convinced you'd rather die moving, than die sitting. Up until now you've never regretted taking a risk. Your only regrets were the ones you didn't take and what might have been. You know well the leprosy of rejection. Your Christian life is made up of mostly perseverance and rolling with the gut punches. But you keep going. Your gut keeps telling you, "If you can drag your weary bones past hell's gate of rejection, you can roll the rest of the way into the arms of the One who can heal all your wounds. And you will feast on the Bread of Life."

The journey becomes lonely when you get close to finding Him. Even leprous friends leave you. You no longer follow the crowds. You push through them. To touch His clothes would be enough now. Like the woman with an issue of blood for twelve years, you are sick of being sick and wonder what it's like to be well again. But where is He? You heard His schedule is to raise Jairus' dead daughter today. You wonder if you can stop Him on His way to make history with you. One touch from Him and you can live through anything.

The Lord is releasing His greatest hunger on earth this hour.

*"And I will shake all nations, and the 'desire' of all nations shall come: and I will fill this house with glory, says the Lord of hosts."* (Haggai 2:7).

That word "desire" means: to crave, hunger, to have a strong longing for. The shaking is making the stomachs of nations to growl, and ours too. I heard He satisfies people with an unsatisfied hunger. I don't know about you, but, "Would you pass me your plate, please?"

# Section Three
# Divine Encounters

# What Uncle Willy's Glass Eye Could See

We called him Uncle Willie. A little old man who sat near the front of the church so he could hear the worship and the message. At times, the Spirit of the Lord would come upon Uncle Willie, causing his frail body to shake and his eyes to weep. Uncle Willie's glass eye intrigued everyone. I'm convinced some came to church just to see it. When He began to shake and weep, his glass eye would often pop out, and if you watched closely, you could see him catching it in his hands. He'd then tilt his head back as though nothing unusual had happened and roll the glass eye back into place.

I soon discovered Uncle Willie could see better than any of us. It happened when a young boy drowned in our hometown river. The river was searched for days without closure for the grieving family. Uncle Willie mentioned to someone, "I know where that body is, I can see it in the bottom of that river."

Word got to the parents and spread quickly to the rescue team. They helped Uncle Willie into a boat and started moving out on the water. Willie's crackling voice steered the rescue team in spite of the boat filling up with doubt. Finally, further downstream, Willie pointed, "The body is right down there." The doubtful crew threw the weighted hook, and sure enough, it hooked the little boy's body. A tainted, saddened cry of relief and wonderment was heard by those on shore, including the parents.

I have been praying recently to know God like never before. While praying, I remembered Uncle Willie with the glass eye.

He saw what others could not see. He heard what no one else could hear. He heard the Father tell him where the body was. I cried, "Lord, I want to see what Uncle Willie could see. He could hear Your voice when others couldn't. I want to see and hear like Uncle Willie. I want to see the lost and dying and find those spiritually dead who have no hope of being found."

With this heart cry I began to expect to hear and see people like I have never seen them before. I have seen too many people as trees walking, and now I expect to see each one clearly (see Mark 8:22-25.). To my surprise it is happening.

This morning I stopped by a branch of my bank that I rarely stop at. I usually use the drive through, but today I felt impressed to go inside. When I looked at the young male teller I heard the word "promotion" and had a witness in my spirit. I played it safe and asked him a question. "Does your job allow you to climb up the ladder?" He said, "Yes." I said to him, "I sense you are going to be promoted on your job." Looking surprised, he responded, "I am getting a promotion next month!" I told him I sensed the Lord telling me that His hand was on his life and He knew where he was. "Your promotion is coming from the Lord," I said. As I walked out of that bank I said to the Lord, "This is fun! Serious fun. Who's next?"

*Lord, forgive us for having eyes to see but not seeing, and ears to hear and not hearing. "But blessed are your eyes, for they see: and your ears, for they hear." (Matthew 13:16).*

# Being Hidden: The Makings of a
# Spiritual Sniper

Does it seem like you are in a hidden place with darkness all around you? And is the enemy breathing down your neck? Be encouraged. You may have the makings of a spiritual sniper. *A Sniper is a skilled military shooter detailed to spot and pick off enemy soldiers from a concealed place.* Snipers are concealed by darkness in the time of war, close to enemy territory. If you can't see daylight, you may be right on schedule. Darkness brings out a sniper's full potential. "We Own The Night!" is their motto. Not many of God's people can stand being hidden for long periods of time. It's a lonely, dark place – but you are not alone. God is with you, and He's creating something powerful out of you. The Lord is saying to many: "The enemy will soon know why you haven't been heard from as of yet. He will soon wonder where you came from. Treasure your hiddenness. It's your advantage. And don't fear the darkness. Your hardships and enemies have come to train you. Don't go AWOL! The moment you were born for is coming. Your light will pierce darkness. My spiritual snipers are coming forth in this season of war."

Although hidden, you must have clear communication with God and your comrades. You must learn the weapon of silence to hear. Silence makes the enemy wonder what you are up to while God is giving you strategy. Silence enables you to hear not only God's still small voice but also the enemy's next plan of attack. I sense the Lord saying, "I'm corporately anointing your ears to hear and eyes to see what no other generation has ever heard or seen for this end time spiritual war. Keep in communication with one another. At times your comrades will be your eyes and ears. It's the lifeline to win. Communicate even if you don't agree. Communicate until you do. You are a team, and no one goes anywhere without each other. A team that can move as one is a dominating force. Laying down your life for each other is not a question. You are no longer considered your own."

## Maneuvering Offensively

> *"From the days of John the Baptist until now, the Kingdom of Heaven has been suffering violence, and the violent have been seizing it by force."* (Matthew 11:12 HCSB).

A former sniper shared with me how he was sent ahead of his troop and how he concealed himself close to the enemy. He said, "A vacant building or any forsaken covering gave me an edge for my deadly aim." He also said, "I became a terror to the terrorists. I could paralyze a large troop with one fatal shot to their comrades. Terror would grip them, for they didn't know where I was. At times I shot from a window of a forsaken building and then ran. If they suspected where I was they would immediately launch heavy artillery into that place. Bounties were placed on my head." I asked him, "Were you afraid of dying?" He said, "No, I died when I left home. If I had any fear in me, I wouldn't have survived what I went through."

His words, "I died when I left home," pierced me. I wonder how many of us realize the day we gave our life to Jesus Christ was the day we died to ourselves, and He now lives in us. *"It is no longer I who live, but Christ lives in me"* (Galatians 2:20 NKJV). And Jesus is never afraid. Having been through much warfare myself, I'm learning when I feel intimidated by the enemy, the truth is: that's really when he is terrified of me. So I move beyond what intimidates me and find sweet victory.

## Staying Focused

Many will see other comrades being elevated this season. Don't be jealous or envious. They are being called to the front line where increased danger lies. Their advancement is your protection. It's a most dangerous time to compare ourselves with one another. Some will think that their strong anointing that's promoting them lessens their need for their comrades or those in authority over them. It actually increases your need for them.

You may seem to be ahead of them in rank, but they are behind you to cover your back. If left alone with our increased anointings, we become dangerous to ourselves and others. This often results in "friendly fire." We need our comrades to keep speaking into our lives to adjust and sharpen our spiritual gifts and weapons so we stay effective. Our training never ends. God will always have someone over us to learn from and someone under us to teach what we are learning.

## Biblical "Sniper" Weapons

*For the weapons of our warfare are not carnal, but mighty through God to the pulling down of strongholds."* (2 Corinthians 10:4).

Throughout history, we've seen snipers rise from obscurity to win wars. One person stands out to me as the greatest sniper in the Bible; David, a shepherd boy, hidden in the hillsides of Judea. Trained by a bear and a lion, he makes his debut with a giant named Goliath. David becomes a sniper in the eyes of the Philistine army as he takes out Goliath with a slingshot and stone. He knew that giant would look good on his resume.

*"Blessed be the LORD my strength, which teacheth my hands to war, and my fingers to fight."* (Psalm 144:1).

David was also a warrior as a scribe. His writings still pierce the darkness in our lives today. The Lord is releasing a scribe anointing upon many for new songs, books, and movies to be written to dismantle powers of darkness upon the earth. Pick up your pen and fight! David's greatest weapon in his arsenal was worship. David was a full-time worshiper and part-time shepherd. He worshiped in secret, and God met him on the battlefield. Worship didn't keep David away from trouble. Worship brought God down into the troubles, and God never lost a battle. In the wars that rage against us today, our greatest weapon is still to worship God in the midst of chaos. Through worship, Heaven comes and fills us with His love and presence, which can touch our worst enemies, causing them to surrender all to Jesus. Loving our enemies keeps them from getting inside of us. We will be facing giants in the days to come. Don't leave home without your slingshot. Remember, as a Believer, Jesus lives in you, and He is not afraid. Besides, you died when you left home.

Welcome, Sniper.

# "I Will Begin to Manifest Myself Alive at the Wailing Wall!"

"O Israel, Your 'Wailing' Wall Shall Become a 'Hailing' Wall." To "wail" means to cry out with lament or grief. To "hail" means to salute, greet, or acclaim enthusiastically, such as, "Hail, King of the Jews!" In the Spirit, I saw the Shekinah Glory of God begin to pierce through the cracks of the Wailing Wall. "Homecoming angels" on the wall were stuffing love notes into every crack as they were imparting revelation into the minds and hearts of the "standing room only" multitude. God's chosen people were now facing the answers to their prayers!

Blinders began dropping off their eyes as the Wailing Wall appeared to be turning into a giant theater screen. Many began to see visions of the King of Kings and Lord of Lords in all of His Glory... in 3-D technicolor! In the Spirit, these panoramic scenes on the wall could be seen by the Jewish people all around the world. A homesick kind of feeling began to spread in epidemic proportion in the hearts of God's chosen people, turning their hearts toward home! God would not force His people to return home, but He did have 'a ways and means' committee to help make them willing to go!

In the Spirit, I sensed great earth-shaking events were now being pre-approved by the Father. These events will cause a great nest-stirring for God's people, the Jews, to be willing to leave where they had grown comfortable, living in seemingly secure places of the earth. But I saw a great shaking in the world's economy coming that would literally gouge the side out of their

Titanic-like financial investments and businesses. I sensed the Father conversing with the angels on this saying, "Yes, that will do it!"

**"Synagogues were being revisited by the greatest teacher ever, Jesus Christ, revealing Himself through scripture as their Messiah — "The King of the Jews!"**

In the Spirit, I saw angels setting up camp around Jewish synagogues and Jesus Himself walking right through many synagogue doors into the midst of their ceremonies. I also saw Him stand up in their midst and read and proclaim, once again, Isaiah 61. But this time, He read the whole chapter, as many of their ears and eyes began to pop open! To many, Jesus began to show Himself openly. Some were having visions; others were actually seeing Him!

I saw children dancing in the streets of Jerusalem.

*"And the streets of the city of Jerusalem shall be full of boys and girls playing in the streets thereof."* (Zechariah 8:5).

At first, it appeared that they were dancing with a make-believe friend. I then saw Jesus laughing and twirling them in the air and catching them as they danced together. The joy of the Lord began running down through the streets of Jerusalem and beyond! Parents of these small children began to experience the presence of God as children began to talk about their experiences, visions, and encounters with Jesus Christ, proclaiming Him to be their Messiah! Children were bringing His anointing and carrying His Glory into their families!

I sense the Father saying, "The intercession of nations for Israel is beginning to be heard, creating the greatest move of My Spirit in all of history in the lives of My chosen people, the Jews. Intercession must increase and prevail to bring My people home."

# Section Four

# Signs of the Times

# A Year When Passions for Jesus Will Run Wild

Passion is a strong and barely controllable emotion.

We are about to see the fulfillment of the song: *'A Soul on Fire'* by Third Day.[2] This song is prophetic at this time. As an ungodly passion for sin accelerates in a world gone crazy, so will an "unquenchable passion for God" begin to burn and run wild in the hearts of many. People will literally catch on fire for God. Some of God's people will be seen as flames of fire walking in malls and grocery stores. This fire will be contagious. In the blink of an eye lost souls will ignite and burn like torches as the fire of repentance explodes within them. Their changed lives will shock the world. Some reports of places being on fire will actually be the result of God's people gathering and worshiping the Lord.

Imaginations of what God can do will run wild, burning in the hearts of many. The call of God will consume people with creative ideas and ways to lift Jesus higher and touch the world. If you paint, watch for your paintings to cause the hearts of observers to burn within them. Some paintings will ignite themselves and burn a trail of repentance across the earth as they go worldwide being noticed by the media. If you write, some writers will discover their writing paper as though holes had been burnt through it. Pens will be catching on fire as though

2 Third Day, *A Soul on Fire;* 2015, Lead Us Back: Songs of Worship Album, Lyrics © Sony/ATV Music Publishing.

they are burning the hands of their writers. If you sing, watch for deliverance as demons flee from the fire of God that is greater than Hell.

# A Kairos Moment - the Appointed Time in the Purpose of God; the Time When God Acts

We have entered a unique kairos moment. God has heard our cries for, "Why not now? Why not here?" Godly secrets of hearts will be manifested. Our moment to change history has arrived. I sense strongly a couple of those God-moments taking place on the earth. For one, there will be those who will change history with a pen. An innocent pen will become the axis that will turn the world upside down and birth a nation in a day (see Isaiah 66:8).

> *"And there are also many other things which Jesus did, the which, if they should be written every one, I suppose that even the world itself could not contain the books that should be written."* (John 21:25).

And the other one will be many who have wept long, lonely nights will discover that their tears were seeds of flowers that are now blooming for their wedding day. Many will discover their once-in-a-life time moment and why they were born. The door is open!

> *"I know thy works: behold, I have set before thee an open door, and no man can shut it: for thou hast a little strength, and hast kept my word, and hast not denied my name."* (Revelation 3:8).

# Angels Were Conversing: "Earth Hasn't Seen Anything Yet!"

As angels were shooting fiery arrows onto the earth, sidewalks and gutters in the streets caught on fire. These arrows of deliverance began hitting the homeless and red light districts of the world. Heaven's aim was precise.

Prison bars were melting and grave clothes were being burned off those held captive in spiritual cemeteries. These fiery arrows then ricocheted and began piercing every denomination and even Spirit-filled churches. Angels were conversing, "Earth hasn't seen anything yet!"

*"In the last days, God says, I will pour out my Spirit on all people. Your sons and daughters will prophesy, your young men will see visions, your old men will dream dreams."* (Acts 2:17 NIV).

# I Am Awakening Your Children and Grandchildren

The enemy is about to hear from our children and grandchildren beginning this season. Watch and expect the passion for Christ to run wild like a raging fire inside of them.

The Lord has allowed them to be placed in strategic locations in the earth and even in some unusual places where we think they shouldn't be; in prisons, homeless on the streets, or wherever they are being held in Satan's grip. They have now been divinely positioned to become a firebrand in God's hand to ignite and explode like dynamite inside the camp of the enemy! This is why the enemy forever has fought against marriages. He feared concerning the Godly seed that was about to come upon the earth to do him in. And here they come!

*"Your descendants will defeat their enemies."*
(Genesis 22:17 The Message Bible).

# A Boomerang Engraved With 'Let My Children Go!' Has Returned

Throughout biblical and recorded history, whenever God was about to do something big in a nation to rescue His people, the enemy would target the babies from being born and attack young children from fulfilling their destiny. Somehow the enemy had an inkling that from these young ones 'deliverers' of nations would come. He, the enemy, tried to thwart the delivery of deliverers...BUT GOD!

Their divine innate gifting was reason enough for the devil's attack, but the greater the enemy's assault, the greater the revelation of God's glory. I sensed the Lord saying, "I will use the abused! Here come the cures for certain terminal diseases. Here come world renowned-doctors, great leaders in governments, Davidic musicians and worshipers, songwriters, singers with angelic bands accompanying them. Here Come the children!"

The war against children has boomeranged. Heaven's blood hounds have now been released, picking up the scent of the blood of Jesus prayed over children. The boomerang had struck terror in the enemy's camp in the darkest nation first, then ricocheted worldwide. Hell's trophy of sex trafficking was on the boomerang's radar.

## Thailand's Quiver Is Full and Shaking With Power

The word came like a knife penetrating the belly of hell concerning Thailand. "I'll be home with bells on!" Angels were placing bells into the trembling hands of children tormented by darkness. Bells started ringing. An irrevocable sound bombarding Thailand had come, shaking that nation with the vengeance of the Lord. Midwives, like angels unaware, were being called from the nations. They began arriving to deliver these young children full-term into their destinies. Bells of freedom were ringing throughout the land. Thailand heard them and her face began to change. Mountains broke forth with singing and the trees of the field clapped their hands as a monumental treasure chest was opened revealing the riches of her inheritance in the earth. Natural as well as spiritual riches, hidden in secret places, were unearthed. Children once in bondage rose from the gutters, singing and dancing on the heels of injustice. These children began invading whole cities. Approaching their city gates, their bold arrow-like proclamations struck the very heart of their enemies. *"The gates of hell shall not prevail against us".* We are still here and now increasing.

> *"Greater is He who is in us than he that is in the world!"* (1John 4:4).

The bells in Thailand were heard worldwide. The enemy's war against children had boomeranged. I sensed the Lord saying, "I am unleashing young children with the call and anointing of Daniel, Elijah, Deborah & Esther, along with their angels into their nations." I see the enemy trembling with questions, "Where are these children so young, yet so dangerous, coming from? Have they come to turn the world upside down? And why at this time?"

> *"But Jesus called the children to him and said, 'Let the little children come to me, and do not hinder them, for the kingdom of God belongs to such as these'"* (Luke 18:16 NIV).

# The Crack in The Liberty Bell

Recently I was revisited with a vision I had of our nation in 1996. Out of nowhere, came a vision of the Liberty Bell. My attention was naturally drawn to the crack in the bell. I was grieved in my spirit that such a deep, fatal crack signified a breach in the true liberty and freedom of our nation. Could that breach ever be repaired? Why wasn't at least the physical defect of the Bell ever filled in with more metal? Could the bell's scar be prophetic, representing our nation's fatal epitaph–unchangeable like the Grand Canyon engraved into Arizona. If only the crack was not there. I felt mesmerized by it. For the longest time my eyes were fixed and I was unable to blink.

Then suddenly, as though in the twinkling of an eye, the brightest light pierced through that crack like a dam bursting. My head immediately turned away from the brightness emanating out of that crack. Instantly, I had a knowing that this was the very Shekinah Glory of God.

Looking away from its brightness, I saw a large rope that was attached to the bell. This rope was intertwined and braided. It seemed to be made out of the prayers and intercessions of God's people. The Hand of the Lord began to reach down towards this rope and grabbed hold of it. The Lord then spoke. "This Liberty Bell is going to ring again." I then remembered the words inscribed on that bell: *"Proclaim Liberty throughout the land and to all the inhabitants thereof."* It was now a rhema word from God.

In the Spirit I had a knowing that the Liberty Bell would be heard again spiritually throughout Philadelphia and across the nation. And with the sound of Liberty, the Shekinah Glory of God would begin to rise up out of obscurity and be seen even in the gross dark places of our nation. Concerning this vision the Lord spoke, "Have My people forgotten that all things are possible?" Tradition holds that the bell cracked while it was being rung during a funeral service in memory of a sheriff. Prophetically, it will ring again for the life and the Glory of a King who still lives in our land. Can you hear the bell ringing?

# I Am Going to Redeem the Times That You Said, "NO!" To Me

I believe we all have missed one of those golden opportunities that we said "no" to because we allowed ourselves to be led by feelings instead of faith. Can our disobedience ever be redeemed? Recently, I blew a silver trumpet to open up a meeting. The Lord showed me that "silver" represents "redemption." When I blew that silver trumpet, I sensed the Lord saying: "I am going to redeem the times that you said, 'No!' to Me! I am going to give you other opportunities! Opportunities that are going to cause you to forget your regrets."

When I look at you, I see no regrets, for there are other opportunities I am bringing your way. And if you will say 'yes' to these opportunities and follow through, it will produce a hundred-fold harvest, more fruit than they would have yesterday or in years gone by.

The Lord says, "This is a turn-around day! This is your turn-around day! I am going to turn things around for you. I am going to turn many of you around who have said 'NO' to Me to say 'YES' with joy. For you are now going to delight to do My will. Forget the past. Your past is not your present. The winter is over and gone. What has been working against you in the past is now going to work for you! Rejoice, for I have greater opportunities coming for you now, more than ever before. These opportunities will restore to you the years the cankerworm and palmerworm have eaten from you."

*"For the gifts and the calling of God are irrevocable."* (Romans 11:29 NKJV).

# I Heard The Lord Say, "I Weep For This World, Yet There's Excitement In My Tears."

I have been feeling overwhelmed at the exceedingly sinful course this world has taken; a collision course with something, somewhere. But during my worship time I heard the Lord say, "I'm excited!" I said, "Lord, what did you say?" He said, "I'm excited!" I said, "How could you be excited? All I see is chaos and gross darkness." He said, "I don't waste chaos. And I don't waste gross darkness. I use them."

"From your perspective the world looks like it's falling apart. From mine it's a grieving, but a wonderful sight. I see treasures in the darkness and greater treasures to come forth from the gross darkness. Weren't you praying for your light to shine brighter? Stay focused on Me and your light will increase to see the treasures I see."

He then said, "Son, you are right. This world is on a collision course. It's on a collision course with the greatest outpouring of My Spirit. The earth is coming into its fullness for harvest. And for that, there's excitement in My tears."

*"All nations will come to your light; mighty kings will come to see your radiance."* (Isaiah 60:3 NLT).

# I Saw a Huge Rusty Plow Sitting in Many Churches

I saw a huge rusty plow sitting in the sanctuary of many churches. It filled the area from the entrance of the sanctuary to the pulpit. Its pointed blade, now dull, rested just short of the altar. The plow seemed ancient and out of place, like it should be in a museum. It struggled to remember the glory days when plowing was crucial in the Kingdom of Heaven. For without plowing there can be no planting, and therefore no harvest. The plow knew it was never meant to be in one place this long.

Suddenly, a knock came pounding on the door of these churches. A knock so powerful that it shifted the huge rusty plow forward enough to touch the altar. I could then see that this huge plow was made up of the congregation as a spirit of intercession came upon it. The spirit of prayer shook the whole house as fresh heavenly oil began dripping down upon this rusty plow.

The Lord then spoke, "As in the days of old, I am returning to this house with great power to bring in the harvest." Immediately, confidence came upon the plow as the congregation proclaimed, "I can do this. I can do that. I can do all things through Christ who strengthens me." A get-up-and-go had come upon us. A pioneering spirit was rising up to take us where we had never gone before; outside to unknown territories and regions where awesome adventure had been waiting for us. We were about to make history.

## Who Was that Knocking on the Door?

I asked the Lord, "Who was that pounding on the door of these churches?" He said, "It's the lost knocking to get inside My house. But the huge rusty plow was taking up all the room and they couldn't get in. Not one of them. But now with My oil dripping on the plow and the shaking moving it forward to outside the house, a great harvest is guaranteed with acceleration. So much so that the plowman will overtake the reaper. (See Amos 9:13.) Churches will be filled again with standing room only. People will line the streets to get in as that well-oiled machine moves outside of My house. I will continue to help by shaking the heavens and the earth, releasing My reverent fear into communities and nations. I will continue to get people's attention, for I want no one to be lost. My shaking alone will cause hardened children and grandchildren to run like prodigals into the arms of Jesus."

I used to think to plow the ground first was a long hard season, and then to wait for the harvest was another long season. But I believe Amos 9:13 is saying that the reaping will be in the same season as we are plowing. In fact, we will overtake the reaper. That's acceleration. The plow was V-shaped, having two huge sides on it. The V-shape reminded me how geese fly and how they partner working together, going forward even in adverse winds.

> *"He that observeth the wind shall not sow; and he that regardeth the clouds shall not reap. As thou knowest not what is the way of the Spirit...even so thou knowest not the works of God who maketh all. In the morning sow thy seed, and in the evening withhold not thine hand: for thou knowest not whether shall prosper, either this or that, or whether they both shall be alike good."* (Ecclesiastes 11:4-6).

## My Hand is Coming Upon Your Plow

"The blood, sweat, and tears that you have sown will now catapult you to find your joy and strength in the harvest fields;

in crack houses, human-trafficking, in fields of addiction, and in the company of man slayers. Where fear abounds, you will discover you are well able to take down every giant in the land. For My hand is now coming upon your plow. I am releasing an electrifying jump start upon it. It is now unstoppable. Don't look back. Don't even look ahead. Look up, for I now go before you and I have your back covered."

## Redemption is Coming upon Your Fields

"Know that your labor until now is not in vain, and though in times past you were weary in well doing, you will be glad you didn't quit. For I am coming onto your fields of labor with redemption. New anointings and unctions will open up new ground and opportunities, for the earth is Mine. Joy will be found in the plowing along with the reaping."

I found this short sermon by Charles Spurgeon to be interesting: "If a farmer knew that a bad year was coming he would perhaps only sow an acre or two; but if some prophet could tell him, 'Farmer, there will be such a harvest next year as there never was,' he would say, 'I will plough up my grass lands, I will stub up those hedges: every inch of ground I will sow.'

So do you. There is a wondrous harvest coming. Plough up your headlands; root up your hedges; break up your fallow ground, and sow, even amongst the thorns. Ye know not which shall prosper, this or that; but ye may hope that they shall be alike good. Enlarged effort should always follow an increased hope of success."

It's time to plow.

# The Lord Said, "There Will Soon Be an Explosion of My Power!"

I said to the Lord on Sunday morning, "The gunshots we are hearing daily on the news are so grieving." The Lord said, "There will soon be an explosion of My power that will be heard around the world that will bring salvation to everyone who believes: first to the Jew, then to the Gentile. This explosion will interrupt news reporters and the media." What I sense I am seeing is only a part of what this explosion will do. A great light will accompany this explosion, piercing gross darkness in the hearts of men. This explosive power will blow the scales off the eyes of the Jewish people and they will run like prodigals to the mountain of the Lord. The sound of a Shofar will roar like a lion calling them home.

This great light will penetrate war zones releasing the angel armies to war with Heaven's most powerful weapon; God's love. I heard that familiar voice conversing with terrorists saying, "Why do you persecute Me?" (see Acts 9:4.) Some angels were causing guns to jam and bullets to disappear as a light brighter than the sun brought instant healing to their hateful hearts. Certain areas of war zones became "fields of altars" as many blinded by the light were crying out, "Lord, what would You have me to do?" Many were surrendering to the Lord on the battlefield.

Angels were protecting some of these soldiers until the light broke through. Some died in battle, but as that bright light shone on their corpse, it was like someone had breathed life back into them and they stood knowing they were a new creature. Hatred was gone and God's love had come. Soldiers on both sides of the battlefield were being visited. Some soldiers seeing their comrades die, then rise, were in shock as the fear of the Lord came upon them. At first, the enemy tried his best to keep these testimonies as quiet as possible. But all the demons and powers of Hell could no longer hold them back. For they were now overcoming the enemy by the Blood of the Lamb and the word of their testimony. Journalists and news reporters at first were struck with unbelief as these miracles began to reach their ears. But as they kept hearing these unusual events, belief began eroding their doubts as soldiers reported seeing Jesus and were being healed of their battle wounds. Curiosity caused many journalists and reporters to listen to the rest of their stories. Slowly but surely these unbelievable testimonies began breaking into the media and news outlets, touching the viewers and the readers with late breaking news that could no longer be ignored.

I asked the Lord, "What caused this shift and turning in the hearts of men?" He said, "It's the prayers of My remnant in the earth who are praying with forgiveness in their hearts and blessing their enemies in a time of being persecuted for My namesake, because that is My will. Praying, forgiving and blessing releases My Spirit to move on anyone. Many of My people have chosen which enemies to pray for and have decided which enemies are too far gone to be saved. But those who are filled with My love know that the real enemy is satan, not flesh and blood; therefore, no one is too far gone."

If you think the terrorists are too far gone, read the story of Saul in Acts 9, whose name was changed to Paul, who wrote much of the New Testament. God wants to change many more names! "Keep praying, keep forgiving, and keep blessing in My name. The fuse has been lit."

# Section Five

# Lessons from Everyday Life

# Have You Considered Walking On Water?

The enemy is always competing for our attention. In the Spirit I heard him accuse us to the Father. "I bet when the storm gets overwhelming, they will stop worshiping You." The Father answered, "No way! I know them. They will worship Me anyhow. If their ship goes under, they will walk on water. They are water walkers! They are storm chasers! They chase storms! The raging sea becomes their sidewalk to get to where I am. They are full-time worshipers, part-time anything else! Their worship brings Me to them."

What if the storm that threatens your life today has come to promote you? Have you considered walking on water? Jesus used a storm at sea to illustrate to His disciples a life lesson: "How to walk on stormy seas". Only one out of twelve was listening. "The first thing that must take place is a strong enough storm that relentlessly batters your ship. The second event: 'How to get your feet wet.' And the grand finale: 'Just do it!' I will take over from there" (My paraphrase, see Matthew 14:22-33.). Once your toes touch the water, whatever was over your head is now under your feet. The storm has weakened. You have worn it out. You have outlasted it and are now up for promotion. The storm that came to destroy you had a spiritual upgrade attached. You now have a testimony with authority to storm the gates of Hell. You have become the perfect storm in satan's kingdom. And there's no water in Hell for him to walk on!

All my storms come without warning. I am never ready for them. But they have one thing in common: I find Jesus in them.

Whether He calls me to walk through the storm or wait for the eye of it: "I know the master of the wind. I know the maker of the rain" (song by Bill Gaither).[3] He can calm the storm or calm me in it.

> *"He lays the beams of His upper chambers in the waters; He makes the clouds His chariot; He walks upon the wings of the wind;"* (Psalm 104:3 NASB).

> *"...What manner of man is this, that even the winds and the sea obey Him!"* (Matthew 8:27).

Ship or no ship: I will worship Him.

---

3  Gaither, Bill, 1984, *I Know the Master of the Wind* written by Joel Hemphill; Heartwarming Records.

# It's Boomerang Time

The gallows built by the enemy to destroy us through sickness will now see cancer, heart disease, high blood pressure, glaucoma, sugar diabetes, and every infirmity under the Son hanging on it. It's boomerang time. We are now being attacked by healing! Receive yours now.

If you have prayed and have not seen healings over a long period of time and you are convinced that you must not have the gift of healing, you decide to stop praying for people. What you don't know is that is your sweet spot. That's the perfect time to pray for one more person. That's when you will start seeing results. This is where healing begins. Think about this. Who wants you to stop praying for people to be healed? Is it the devil or the Lord?

I was in Lowe's walking around and I overheard a lady telling someone how sick she was with a sinus infection. As I kept walking the Lord spoke to me to go and pray for her. I said, "Lord, I'm not used to praying for people in public." The Lord said, "I am. Most of my ministry of healing and deliverance was in public, not in the temple. Another thing, it's not about you, but about me. I just want you to be a vessel to give me a chance to touch her. If she doesn't get healed it won't be your fault. And if she does get healed, it won't be because of you either. I just want you to give Me a chance to heal her."

I stepped out and asked her if I could pray for her. She said, "Yes, I have had this sinus infection for many years and have had two surgeries and it still comes back often." I prayed and asked the Holy Spirit to come upon her and I took authority over this infirmity to leave her. I felt the Lord's presence. She appeared to not feel anything, so I told her, "Sometimes God heals immediately and other times gradually." As I walked away, I felt a healing witness go through my own body. Perhaps being a vessel for Him opens ourselves up to be touched, as well as others. I said, "Lord, what does that witness mean that ran through me in spite of no evidence of that lady's healing?" He said, "That's the dam of healing building up inside of you for the next person who needs prayer."

# If Nobody Prays, Nobody Gets Healed

On the way to minister at a church recently I sensed the Lord saying, "I want to heal someone at the very start of your message." I thought that is strange for me in my meetings; I didn't think I had a healing ministry. As I sat down right before the service I heard people around me talking about their physical problems, medicines they were taking and doctor reports that concerned them.

I kept thinking, which was my downfall. If I get up and say that God wants to heal someone before I speak and if I didn't hear correctly and no one gets healed it will be a terrible way to begin these two nights of meetings. I am ashamed to tell you that I didn't go with it. I started my message and played it safe.

At the end of the service, as always, I invited people forward for special prayer. One woman came before me with her body shaking. She said, "I just got out of the hospital. I had a stroke and my heart is so weak the doctor said there is nothing more they can do. I could die any minute. When she spoke those words, any faith I had left me. I felt so helpless for her. I anointed her with oil and laid my faithless hands on her head. I know I prayed in unbelief hoping she wouldn't die with my hand on her head. I was just glad to see her still alive as she left the meeting later.

The next morning I got a phone call from a pastor who was in the service. He said, "Brother Bill, the woman you prayed for with the bad heart called me this morning. She said she woke up feeling fine. Her heart feels great, her blood pressure and diabetes numbers are normal. I said, "That is awesome!" I didn't tell him, but I knew something. I had nothing to do with that healing; it was all God. I then realized since I had nothing to do with it, I am going to step out more because it's not about me. We're just conduits that God wants to flow through.

I was eating breakfast one morning at a restaurant and overheard a woman talking about going for her chemo treatment. I felt that little nudge to go and ask her if I could pray for her. Immediately, the devil said to me, "Who do you think you are?" I said to him, "Who do you think God is?" I stood up and went over and prayed for her. Again, I am learning if nobody prays, nobody gets healed.

The old hymn, *Channels Only* by Mary E. Maxwell, says it all:

Channels only, blessed Master,
But with all Thy wondrous pow'r
Flowing through us, Thou canst use us
Every day and every hour.[4]

Remember, even Jesus prayed a second time to heal a blind man's eyes. I believe He was establishing the principle of pursuing healing through prayer.

*"Once more Jesus put his hands on the man's eyes. Then his eyes were opened, his sight was restored, and he saw everything clearly."* (Mark 8:25 NIV).

4  Maxwell, Mary E., *Channels Only*. Only information available.

# My Favorite Flower is an Iris

One morning during a three month sabbatical I was walking to my prayer room. I passed by our bay window that was filled with beautiful flowers called Irises. They were in full bloom, shouting a grand finale of colors and majesty. As I walked past them, I heard the Lord whisper, "Bill, I want you to sit down and behold the flowers." As I did, I found myself mesmerized by their beauty and I began to repeat their name out loud... "Iris, Iris, Iris" and then out came, "I Rest!"

It's the first time a flower ever preached to me. I kept gazing upon their glory and studied them. I couldn't find one flower that looked like it was struggling. I couldn't find one flower that looked like it was worried. Have you ever seen a flower that looked worried? (unless you don't water it) These flowers were just being and growing into what God had called them to be with no struggle, no sweat and no worry. They looked like they were rejoicing.

The Lord spoke through those Irises saying. "Bill, I am calling you to rest in Me. As you rest in Me you will naturally grow into all that I've called you to be. There is a rest to them that believe. You not only must believe in Me, but believe Me to bring to pass what I have spoken to you. I am the faithful One who has called you, Who will also do it. Only believe."

*"Come to me, all you who are weary and burdened, and I will give you rest."* (Matthew 11:28 NIV).

# The Bumps on the Road to Glory

I wish one of us five kids on the bike would have seen that bump sign before we started down that hill. But no one saw it. If just one of us had seen it, I wouldn't be wearing this bump on my head today.

I was five years old and extra short for my age. I was in the basket up front. The impact to my head was so hard that doctors discovered it caused a bone to grow abnormally on the right side above my eye. With that bad news came another shocker. The x-ray also showed a brain tumor. I was sent to a brain specialist at Mercy Hospital in Pittsburgh, PA. Mercy Hospital is a Catholic Hospital. My mother got all the nuns and priests praying for me. All I can tell you is the morning of my tumor surgery, my mother came into my hospital room all excited. She said, "Bill, they just took another set of x-rays to make sure they know how to take the tumor out, but they can't find it. It's gone!"

I learned early in life to never tell God who He can't use to bless us, for there are hungry hearts in every church and denomination who we will need in the days ahead. The final blow to that tumor came two years earlier when my mother began to tell everybody, "This is my little preacher!" Years later, the Lord showed me her spoken prophetic word over my life, "This is my little preacher!" ate the tumor alive like a spiritual pack man, for it had come to steal God's purpose for my life. They then did surgery to scrape the bone away on my head as much as they could, but it still marks my life to this day.

Have you ever wished that you could go back one day in your life and live it over? You guessed it. That would have been the one day for me. I would have done anything but take a bike ride. But as I am getting older, with years of wisdom from the school of hard knocks, I am learning to think differently. I don't think I would change a thing. For God blessed the bump in the road that led me straight to Jesus when I was five years old. Looking back, it wasn't the easy road that blessed my life. It was the broken road that blessed me. What about you?

# Big Leagues and Big Hits Go Together

During a Super Bowl game, the kick-off receiver caught the football deep in the end zone and ran like a deer, only to hit a brick wall of opposition at about the 20 yard line. Even the announcer sounded shaken at the sudden impact felt high above the stadium. The receiver held onto the football with a vengeance, and the opposing players' frantic scramble to steal the ball was all in vain. Later in the game, unable to forget this play, I said to the Lord, "Why have I been in a season where I have been taking so many hard hits?" The Lord answered, "Son, I have put you into the big league. Big leagues and big hits go together!"

His words were life to me. The enemy almost convinced me, "God has left you and He doesn't care about you." I thought it was God letting me down when He was actually raising me up. I could see where God was now. He was on the sidelines as my coach.

Could it be when we experience His awesome presence is when we are on the sidelines with Him receiving encouragement and instructions for the next game play? All of a sudden, I felt honored by those hits and assaults from the opposition coming against me. They were now signs and confirmation of my promotion. Many others have been promoted into the big league of God's Kingdom and are unaware of it. When the enemy hits you hard or life itself comes against you, hold onto the football with both hands. Hold onto God's word that He has spoken to you. The enemy's job is to strip the football or God's word from you. And when you get knocked down, get up proudly, for you are in the big leagues and the game is not over.

In another play that same kick-off receiver, Jacoby Jones, caught the football eight yards deep in the end zone and ran all the way for a touchdown, tying a Super Bowl record of the longest kick-off return in Super Bowl history. They first thought it was a record breaker of a hundred and nine yards, but they remeasured the field and found that it tied a previous record. Big leagues and big hits not only go together, but big hits and big scores also go together!

Many reading this message are hitting major bumps in the road and taking some big hits in life. But your bumps have come to bless you and your hits have made you stronger to make history winning touchdowns in God's Kingdom. God is measuring the field for you.

It's time to break the records!

*"Therefore, since we are surrounded by such a huge crowd of witnesses to the life of faith, let us strip off every weight that slows us down, especially the sin that so easily trips us up. And let us run with endurance the race God has set before us."* (Hebrews 12:1 NLT).

# No Fireworks Until It Is Dark Enough

While singing the song, *10,000 Reasons*, this verse gripped me, "Let me be singing when the evening comes." I don't know about you, but I want to be singing when the evening comes. It's easy to sing in the morning, but in the evening it's more difficult when darkness sets in. Did you notice America sees no July 4th fireworks until it is dark enough? I can imagine 10,000 children asking their parents, "Daddy, Mommy, when will the fireworks start?" Parents in vain trying to explain to their children, "It's not dark enough!" I wonder if there's a blessing about darkness that we as God's children don't understand.

Did you notice when the fireworks begin you no longer focused on the dark night, but were mesmerized by the awesome bright lights exploding, sounding like giant boom boxes penetrating the dark sky and shaking the earth? The darkness only enhanced and seemed to energize the fireworks as they danced on heaven's ceiling. As I watched, I sensed the Lord saying, "Bill, that's you! That's My people. The world will begin to see My people like fireworks in their darkest night. I'm setting the stage using the backdrop of gross darkness. So far the world has only heard the enemy play his out of tune instrument since he fell like lighting from heaven. He lost his place in the choir. But I have an orchestra about to be heard from in the nations. And this is the part where My grand finale comes in to be seen and heard. My explosive fireworks will cause multitudes to look up and be in awe, calling them out of darkness. My salvation, healing, deliverance, and glory captivating those in darkness will begin to fall down upon them shaking the earth. Keep singing and worshiping Me as the evening comes. You are My grand finale in the darkness.

> *"Arise, shine; for thy light is come, and the glory of the LORD is risen upon thee."* (Isaiah 60:1).

# At Least Once in a Lifetime We Should Do This…

A commercial on TV shows a father talking to his son at the table. The father says, "So you quit your job and took all your savings and bought a new car. And now you are going to drive across the country." The son says, "Yep, that's my plan." The father stares down at the table and says, "I wish I had done that." The next scene, the son is driving his new car and the father is in the passenger seat sipping a slurpee and looking very content.

I believe in each one of us is God's DNA that longs to take a risk at least once in a lifetime, particularly when it appears very foolish. There are those today who are being challenged by the Lord to put all their eggs in one basket and let the chips fall where they may; to step out into the crazy unknown where it doesn't make a bit of sense, but brings a smile to God's face.

I wonder as those remaining disciples sat in the boat and watched Peter walk on water, if it wasn't one of those 'I wish I had done that' moments that haunted them the rest of their lives. Is God speaking to you today? Is He giving you a once in a lifetime opportunity to do what you've always wanted to do, so you have no regrets of "I wish I had done that?"

*"The master was furious. That's a terrible way to live! It's criminal to live cautiously..."*
(Matthew 25:26, 27 The Message Bible).

# Section Six

# Homeward Bound – The Final Roar

# Her Children Remember

*(L to R) Wayne, Dick (adopted at 7 days old; he went to be with Jesus when He was 39), myself, Jim, Carol, Mom (Gertrude) and Dad (Clifford went to be with Jesus at 85)*

My brother Jim had these words to add as he saw some prophetic signs foreshadowing Mom's entrance into heaven: "As Mother aged near 89 and then 90, she was strong in faith and spirit. Her mind was steadfast on the Lord, family and friends. Still, she was up and down in her earthly vessel day by day, week by week and month by month. It did seem though she would recover from whatever came her way and get back on her feet. She quite often would say, 'I'm just ready to go home to see the Lord, Kick (the nickname for her husband) and my mother.' I felt sure she could sense the nearness of the Lord in many ways. I would say, 'God still has a purpose for you here, so just keep praying for your family and others.'"

Three significant events would note her soon to come transition into Glory, a transition that would seem to allow mom to escape death as the world knows it. First, there was a dream her granddaughter Jamie had twice about Mom's bathroom in the house we grew up in. Later, that would be interpreted as a place of cleansing and making oneself ready to leave.

The second was when I heard a still small voice as I entered into our own family bathroom, "Jim, I'm just waiting for your Mommy to come home." I immediately understood that to be a voice in the spirit sense of her husband Kick, our Dad, who was waiting for her arrival into heaven. That is exactly what he would say many nights as he would gaze out the window at home waiting for Mom to pull into the driveway.

Last but not least, as Mom was in the bathroom getting ready for bed, we were told she was full of laughter and joy. As she walked from the bathroom to her bed, it was as though she laid her body down, and stepped right into Glory.

*"...because through Christ Jesus the law of the Spirit who gives life has set you free from the law of sin and death."* (Romans 8:2 NIV).

My brother Wayne shared this with me: "Since Mom went to heaven, I am reminded of the many things she used to say. I recently lost a job and her words came back to me. 'Take your burden to the Lord and leave it there.' I did and the Lord provided a better job with more money. She taught me to have faith when I pray and believe and not doubt. What she said lives on in me."

My sister Carol shared this - "Mom told me, 'When you get sick, get the oil out and anoint yourself and pray.' Recently

I had a foot injury and I got the oil out. All I had was Crisco oil. I rubbed it on my foot and prayed. I discovered the next day that God had touched my foot. Mom said, 'When you run into problems, trust the Lord and He will see you through.' She would always tell me, 'When I leave this world, don't worry, you'll know where I'll be.' We all know where she is."

# Mom's Shoeless Entry into Heaven

Just hours before mom met Jesus, my sister visited her and said her face was glowing and she couldn't find one wrinkle on it. She was even walking on her own. One of my brothers stopped by also to see her minutes later. I called her around 7:30 pm that evening and she said, "I was going to call you." Her voice was strong and clear. She told me that she had called my other brother Jim and talked to him also. Then within three hours of talking to us children, she left. The last words my brother heard my mother say was: "Tell everyone I love them."

Mom had an unusual request when she left this world. She said, "When they lay me in the casket, I don't want them to put any shoes or socks on me. I want to dance on the streets of gold in my bare feet." I called the funeral director and told him mom's unusual request and why. He agreed. At the funeral someone said to me. "It's going to be hard to fill your mother's shoes." I told them, "She doesn't have any."

# The Awesome Power in A Mother's Mantle

I'm not sure how this works, but I believe a mother's mantle casts a long shadow. I saw my mother's mantle fall during the going away celebration at her church. It then unfurled like a tailor-made garment of love and continued to spread. I believe her mantle is imparting spiritual inheritance to many, even those who never knew her.

Though my mother, Gertrude Yount, has gone to be with Jesus, multitudes have been touched and encouraged by the many healings and miracles that God gave her in this lifetime. But what I will remember the most about mom is her persevering faith in spite of her many hardships. She found God in the storms of life. She touched so many people with God's love in the ninety years she lived. Despite the many healings she experienced, she is now totally healed forever.

She would always tell us. "When I get better, I'm getting my license back." She still blamed the state for taking her license. She told everyone, "They made a mistake about me." I have a gut feeling mom now has her license back. I feel like she's driving something up there; maybe a chariot. "Look out for those speed limit signs, Mom!"

This story seems to sum up the fabric of my mother's prophetic mantle.

A mother had a little daughter playing down the neighborhood. A storm was brewing and the mother called the neighbor and said, "Send my little girl home quick." The little girl started walking home two blocks away as the storm broke loose. A torrential downpour of rain beat the earth as thunder and lightning flashed across the sky. As the mother watched anxiously out her kitchen window, she noticed every time lightning flashed her little girl would stop and start to smile. Several times as lightning flashed her little girl again would stop and a smile would break out on her face. The mother, terrified, ran out of the house and down the sidewalk and picked up her little girl in her arms and ran inside the house. The mother said to the daughter. "Honey, how come every time the lightening flashed, you just stopped and started to smile?" The little girl responded. "Mommy, all the way home God's been taking my picture!" Oh, to have a childlike faith. To know in our worst storm, God is taking our picture. Raise your hands and receive by faith the power in my mother's mantle right now: The gift of faith that only believes and doesn't know how to doubt; the patience that outlasts every storm and God's love that breaks the rules.

Don't forget to smile, because all the way home God is taking your picture!

# A Glimpse of Heaven

I spoke at my mother's church recently. This time she wasn't there. She has moved to another location. She's in her mansion just over the hill top, in that bright land where we'll never grow old. Her new address is 'Glory Hallelujah' along the streets of gold, and she hasn't stopped dancing since she left here. I can hear her saying, "Make sure you get up here. This place is something else. I can't describe it. You'll have to come see it for yourself." I know now what my mother experienced a split second before she left this world. She caught a glimpse of heaven and it took her breath away.

I talked to Mom shortly before she passed. She said, "Bill, I can't tell everyone this for they wouldn't believe it, but I wanted to let you know. I was feeling discouraged and all of a sudden I was in the lap of Jesus. I don't know how I got there. He put His arm around me and I felt the greatest peace I have ever known."

This is one more reason I called Mom almost every day: to see what God was doing in her life. I remember thinking the day would come when I would call her and the phone would ring and there would be no answer. But since the day Mom went to be with Jesus, I have never dialed that number again, not even by mistake. Unspeakable joy has filled me knowing she is fully alive and I will see her again where the roses never fade. I believe the words of this song by Terry Smith (paraphrased by me) describe her joyful anticipation as she waits to see us again:

*I'll be waiting on the far side banks of Jordan*
*I'll be dancing; kickin' up gold dust with your dad*
*And when we see you coming we will jump up with a shout*
*And come running through the shallow waters reaching for*
    *your hand.*[5]

---

5   Smith, Terry, *Far Side Banks of the Jordan;* Published by Warner/Chappell
Music, Inc.

Original Lyrics:  *And I'll Be Waiting On The Far Side Banks Of Jordan*
                *I'll Be Sitting Drawing Pictures In The Sand*
                *And When I See You Coming I Will Rise Up With A Shout*
                *And Come Running Through The Shallow Water*
                *Reaching For Your Hand*

## *Contact the Author*

Blowing the Shofar Ministries
132 E. North Ave.
Hagerstown, MD 21740

E-mail: theshofarhasblown@juno.com

*www.billyount.com*

If you would like to be blessed by the ministry of Bill Yount, please contact him at the above e-mail address. He is available to minister at your church, conference, meeting, coffee house or anyplace God's people are gathered in His Name.